# Suzuki®

## GUITAR SCHOOL

Volume 3
Guitar Part
*International Edition*

AMPV: 1.01

© 2018, 1999 International Suzuki Association
Sole publisher for the entire world except Japan: Summy-Birchard, Inc.
Exclusive print rights administered by Alfred Music
All rights reserved. Printed in USA.

Available in the following formats: Book (0392), Book & CD Kit (42082), CD (0472)

| Book | Book & CD Kit |
|---|---|
| ISBN-10: 0-87487-392-4 | ISBN-10: 1-4706-3507-0 |
| ISBN-13: 978-0-87487-392-4 | ISBN-13: 978-1-4706-3507-7 |

# INTRODUCTION

*FOR THE STUDENT:* This material is part of the worldwide Suzuki Method® of teaching. The companion recording should be used along with this publication. In addition, there are guitar accompaniment part books that go along with this material.

*FOR THE TEACHER:* In order to be an effective Suzuki teacher, ongoing education is encouraged. Each regional Suzuki association provides teacher development for its membership via conferences, institutes, short-term and long-term programs. In order to remain current, you are encouraged to become a member of your regional Suzuki association, and, if not already included, the International Suzuki Association.

*FOR THE PARENT:* Credentials are essential for any Suzuki teacher you choose. We recommend you ask your teacher for his or her credentials, especially those related to training in the Suzuki Method®. The Suzuki Method® experience should foster a positive relationship among the teacher, parent and child. Choosing the right teacher is of utmost importance.

To obtain more information about the Suzuki Association in your region, please contact:

International Suzuki Association
www.internationalsuzuki.org

# CONTENTS

6

Preparation for
# Nonesuch – Anon.

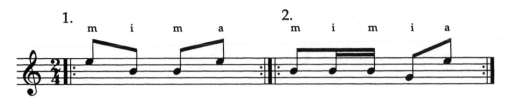

$\boxed{1}$
# Nonesuch

Playford Collection
(England, 17th Century)

# 2
# Greensleeves

Anonymous

# 3
# Packington's Pound

Anonymous

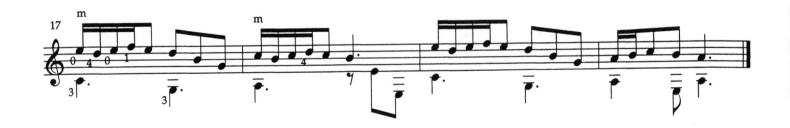

# 4
# Ghiribizzo

N. Paganini

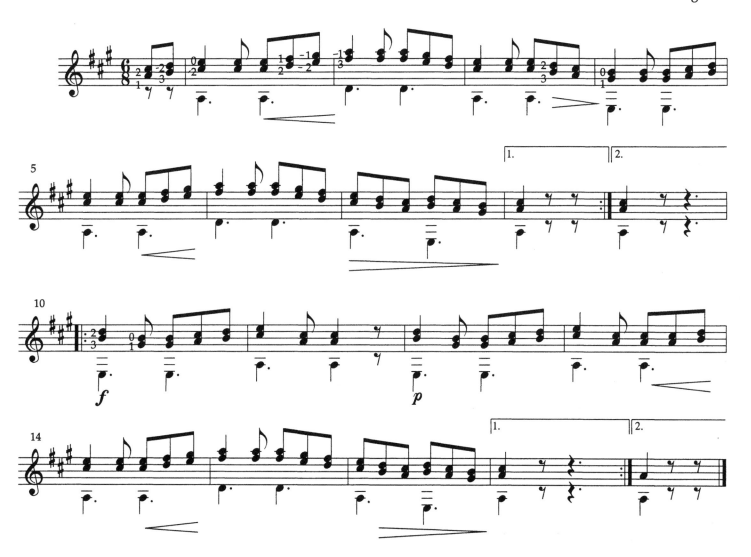

## Preparation for
# Waltz by N. Paganini

# 5
# Waltz
## from Sonata #9

N. Paganini

# 6

## Andantino

F. Carulli

*Fine*

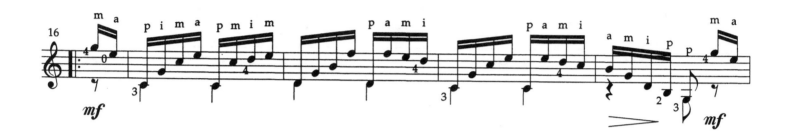

*D. C. al Fine*

# 7
# Calliope
## (Lesson 61)

J. Sagreras

# 8
# Etude

F. Carulli

## Preparation for
# Etude by N. Coste

# 9

# Etude

N. Coste

# 10

# Arietta
## Theme & Variations

Joseph Küffner

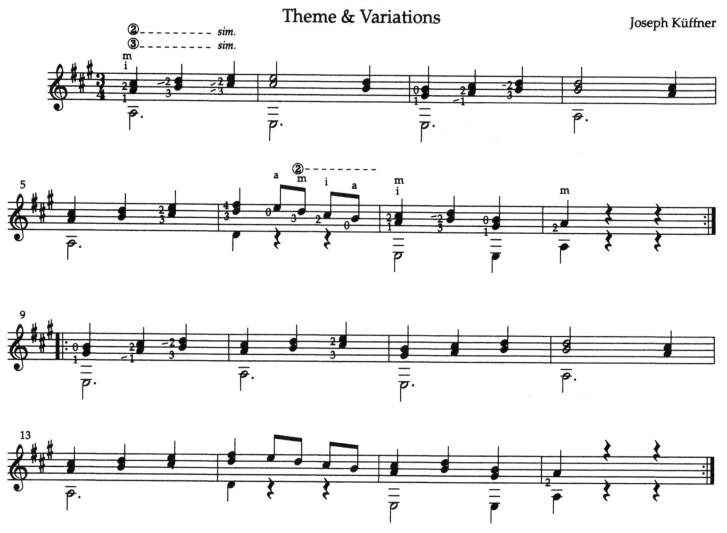

**Variation A**

**Variation B (minore)**

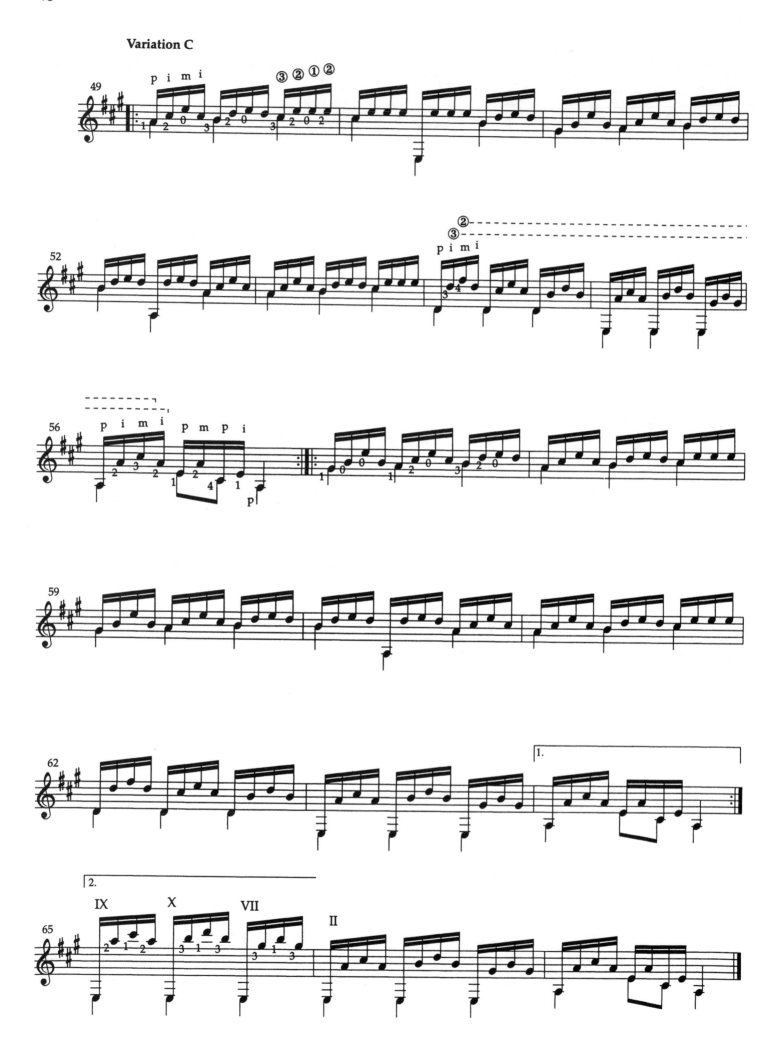

## Preparation for
# Celeste y Blanco by H. Ayala

$\boxed{11}$

# Celeste y Blanco
### (Aire de Cielito)

Hector Ayala

**Tiempo de Vals**

**Tiempo de Gato**

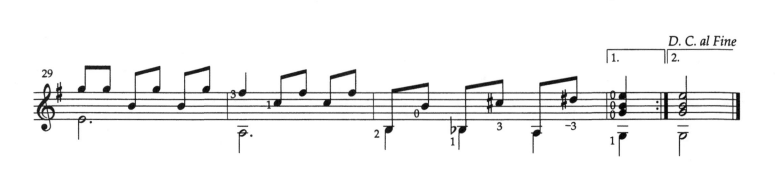